Laymah,

You are E.

Tiffany

THE ESTHER PROJECT

EVERY WOMAN'S GUIDE TO LIVING WITH PASSION AND PURPOSE

TIFFANY M. WILLIAMS

xulon
PRESS

Table of Contents

PREFACE

TIFFANY'S STORY

"" For I know the plans I have for you," declares the Lord, "plans to prosper you and not to harm you, plans to give you hope and a future."
Jeremiah 29:11(NIV)

A Conversation with God

I am often asked, "Why did you create the Esther Project?" Simply put, I was inspired by a conversation with God! After the dissolution of a relationship that I thought would lead to marriage, I resorted to questioning God about the viability of my desire to be a wife and mother. Between cries of "but Lord I'm getting old," and "but God you promised," I heard a distinct reply, "But are you ready?" Without hesitation and before my conscious mind had an opportunity to negotiate, the truth in my heart spoke out and declared a resounding "NO!" The response I received next was, "Well then just get ready."

My personal response to that profound exchange was to get real with myself and catalogue the areas in my life that needed to transform in order to make room for another person in my life and to present myself as a whole person in a lifelong relationship. I realized that I had to be what I wanted to attract. Motivated to action, immediately I decided that I was going to take six months to strategically address each area of my much needed personal development.

A Look in the Mirror

As any good look in the mirror will reveal, there were some very apparent issues that were first priority in my self-care routine or lack thereof. I acknowledged personality traits that were beginning to interfere with my ability to relate to others with vulnerability. My character, or the sum total of my habits, was being challenged and threatened. Although I frequently led, inspired, and encouraged others, I had failed to lead, inspire, and encourage the most important person. I discovered that I had forgotten myself. Somewhere in the expanse of achieving my ultimate career goal of becoming a judge, flourishing in my ministry pursuits, serving others, and being a loving sister, daughter, and friend, I had neglected the foundation of my own existence—my joy. Ironically, the outgoing message on my phone voicemail encourages callers to remember that "The joy of the Lord is your strength!" (Nehemiah 8:10). But I had lost my joy in life, and it was reflecting in my inability to step into the dreams that I had developed for my personal fulfillment.

The Genesis of Transformation

My journey to rediscover my forgotten self began without fanfare and public notification. No Facebook updates, no kick-off party—just a private prayer of dedication to the Lord that I would honor my commitment to "get ready." During my journey, I began with the basics of rededication to self-care which inspired me to revisit the fundamentals of my relationship with God. As I took time to cook again and eat at home (rather than eat every meal out), I used that time to reflect on the day's interactions and the divine purpose by which those interactions impacted my life. I took more time out to allow God into my day by asking for his wisdom and guidance in my daily decision-making. I began reading the biblical book of Proverbs, which revealed to me the value of wisdom – how it informed my choices and thus increased my quality of life. As a result, I noticed other people's needs and focused less on my own. I opened myself up more to some people and closed my inner circle to others, as wisdom so guided. I began to feel differently and look better. My surroundings started to look better as I began to organize my home differently and acquire essentials that I lacked in creating a home. I felt better because I had positive, encouraging, and loving people breathing life into what I thought were dead circumstances. Women of power and authority around me were praying and speaking words of encouragement over my life while demanding that I be all that God created me to be. These were friends and family members with vision and purpose who surrounded me with a safety net of trust and support and inspired me not to play small anymore, but to realize the power within me. Finally, I saw who I was—powerful beyond my own belief.

The Birth of the Esther Project

A few weeks into my personal journey, I had a conversation with a friend who has been like a younger sister to me. As she relayed her own personal desire to transform her present space in life and move forward toward her goals, I was drawn to personally mentor her through her progress. As we exchanged the covenant bond of mentor-mentee, she later sent me a heartfelt text message thanking me for my commitment to help her at this critical juncture. In my response, I encouraged her to think of her journey as a personal "Esther" project—referencing the transformative journey of Queen Esther in the Bible. No truer words were ever expressed!

Simultaneously, I struggled to prepare my remarks for the Women's Empowerment Conference at my church—the Upper Room Full Gospel Church in New Jersey. As the daughter of the founders/pastors and as an associate minister, the pressure was on to deliver a timely word to the sisters attending the conference. Not to mention that I was God's instrument, delivering the message that He would want the women in attendance to hear. I prayed and asked the Lord to reveal a relevant message for the ladies, and I searched my own experiences for the testimony in my own life that I could share. Once again, He answered. I thought about my disappointment and hurt from the failed relationship that was still raw on my emotions. I pondered the personal journey that I had committed to take. And then the words of the conversation with my mentee hit me—a personal Esther project.

I began to study the biblical book of Esther, drawing inspiration from the story of this young woman, taken from obscurity and prepared for a public position of authority and visibility as the new queen. When I reflected on how God used her position as queen for a wholly unrelated, yet transformational, role of saving her fellow Jewish countrymen from genocide, I knew instantly that I had unlocked the chamber to my forgotten self. My forgotten self was a self of purpose, driven to inspire other men and women to fulfill their purpose. I realized that Esther's story was my story—in fact, it was every woman's story. The lessons and inspiration from her journey had the potential to transform every woman in their personal life journey.

Needless to say, I had decided on my remarks for the conference, but I had found something greater. In my continued prayer seeking wisdom and guidance, the Esther Project—an empowerment movement, encouraging women to position themselves to fulfill their purpose—was birthed. Through the journey, women are taught to: 1) de-clutter; 2) master the fundamentals of self-care; 3) live on purpose by enjoying life; 4) expand their territory through relationship building; 5) transform their character by becoming a cocoon in the wilderness; 6) break forth by increasing their emotional and physical strength; and 7) take their position as a leader that can empower others. My vision is that the Esther Project's empowerment movement would impact women globally through the development of Esther Ambassadors and Esther Empowerment Circles throughout the world.

Esther Revealed

The revelation of the location and texture of the part of me that I had forgotten caused me to shout a rallying cry, which has become the mantra of every woman who has embarked on the Esther Project journey— "I am Esther!" Through the birthing of the Esther Project, I am fulfilling my purpose of encouraging and empowering women throughout the world. This dynamic project seeks to transform women's lives into "Esther" daily. My own journey yielded this ministry project, book, and a worldwide network of sisters, mothers, and daughters. More importantly, it empowered me to know that I am fearfully and wonderfully made in the image of God. I am assured that I have a divine destiny of joy and happiness that

I am privileged to experience right now. And yes, the joy of the Lord continues to be my strength! Prepare to take your position for your purpose and keep telling yourself, "I Am Esther!"

CHAPTER 1

ESTHER'S STORY IN A NUTSHELL

"Who knows if perhaps you were made queen for just such a time as this?"
Esther 4:14 (NLT)

The inspiration for The Esther Project is a young Jewish woman named Esther, originally known as Hadassah, who became the Queen of Persia. Esther remains a modern day role model, inspiring contemporary women seeking to move forward toward their own empowerment. Her story inspires women on their perpetual journey of womanhood. Esther's journey is memorialized in the biblical book of Esther and is often noted in historical, biblical, and Judaic based writings. Esther is also the central figure in the Jewish celebration of Purim, a day that commemorates the deliverance of the Jewish inhabitants of ancient Persia from annihilation. Esther resided in the province of Susa with her cousin, Mordecai, who had adopted her after her parents died. She was married to Xerxes, King of the mighty empire of Persia. During Xerxes' reign, Persia grew to be a dominant superpower. He was known as an ambitious warrior king who was anxious to spread his kingdom.

Prior to Esther's reign, Xerxes was wedded to a different queen, Vashti, who fell out of favor with the king when she refused a summons during a celebratory feast. Xerxes was angered at her public insolence and embarrassed at the precedent that her refusal set for other women in the kingdom. Vashti was dismissed and a search for a new queen began. The stage is set. Enter Esther.

After the king decreed the search for a new queen, Esther was taken into the king's palace with other women to prepare for the competitive royal selection process. First, Esther entered into an intensive preparation process where she learned etiquette, grooming, self-care, fashion and wardrobe, the art of conversation, and everything necessary to demonstrate to the king that she would seamlessly acquire the role as queen if selected. During her preparation, Esther was moved to the best place in the harem, given hand maidens, and her choice of clothing and jewelry. Through her mastery of preparation, Esther found favor in the king's eyes and was selected as queen.

During Esther's reign as queen, she hid her Jewish identity because of the status of Jews in the kingdom. Jewish inhabitants were allowed to reside in the kingdom after they had been previously exiled from Jerusalem. However, they did not possess full rights, privileges, and protections of other citizens. Hence, Mordecai advised her to change her Jewish name, Hadassah, to a Babylonian name, Esther.

One of the king's chief advisors, Haman, became jealous of Mordecai and hateful of the Jewish inhabitants because of his prejudice that had been passed down generationally from his Agagite descendants. Haman abused his royal power by devising a plan to mislead Xerxes into signing an ordinance to kill every Jewish inhabitant. Mordecai challenged Esther to intercede on behalf of her countrymen despite the fact that protocol prevented her from approaching the king on any matter uninvited without the risk of death. Ultimately, he challenged Esther to consider whether God had ordained that she had been selected as queen so that she could be in a position to intervene under these circumstances. In other words, Mordecai challenged Esther to consider whether she had been purposed to be queen for "such a time as this" (Esther 4:14).

Esther's response was to fast and pray for guidance in her decision and to entreat her handmaidens and all the Jews in the kingdom to do the same. She decided to risk her life and approach the king to plead for the lives of her people. Esther was successful by using her grace and hospitality, preparing a feast for the king in whose eyes she continued to receive favor. He was so pleased with her that he asked for her request to be made known and offered her up to half of his kingdom. While the king's edict could not be rescinded once it was issued, Esther was able to convince the king to issue an edict that would enable the Jewish inhabitants to use arms to defend themselves if anyone tried to kill them. Esther was also able to expose Haman's racial bias which resulted in his execution as well as the public execution of his ten sons. In Esther's courageous stand, the lives of countless men, women, and children were saved.

Lessons from Esther's journey

Esther had to figure out who she was—either a queen enjoying the comforts of a carefree existence or a woman determined to do God's will at all costs. Mordecai challenged her to be relevant to the needs of the time. Esther's story illustrates that we cannot neglect the responsibility of positions of power that God sets us in. We are called to use our power at just the right time, for the right reason. We have the potential and authority to impact the quality of life of others, which are both a responsibility and a challenge. Did you ever consider that perhaps you are in the circumstances that you are in "for such a time as this?" Esther's story compels the conclusion that she was preordained to be queen during this time so that she could intervene at just the right time. God loved his people so much that He orchestrated the plan that one Jewish young woman would be the highest ranking female leader in the palace through her grace and humility.

Here's some inspiration from Esther's journey:

Get in the game. Esther got in the game. Achieving your purpose requires knowing the rules of the game. God will orchestrate and order everything so that we can step into our roles. He will give you insight in order to have the Godly confidence, determination, and focus demonstrated by Esther. She pushed past those challenges and still got in the game.

Say good night to your past. Esther did not allow her past to hold her back. Nor did she wear her experiences on her sleeve. There were simply no excuses. We are neither defined nor limited by the circumstances that we find ourselves in. As an orphan, God did not intend to break her or limit her ability to have a successful relationship. It was intended to bring out the gifts inside of her.

Purpose requires preparation. Esther prepared herself. Preparation can be painful because we are getting out of our comfort zone, allowing us to overcome lameness, sameness, and tameness. We define ourselves by our past sometimes—material possessions, family background, socio-economic status. But these are worldly attributes that society assigns. God already knows who you are and wants you to know who you are. He gives us signs that we are royalty and victorious.

Keep it positive. Esther had a positive attitude and submitted to the process. She exhibited openness to being transformed. Her attitude was one of mastering her craft of personal presentation. Her mind allowed her to see herself as queen, and as a result, Esther excelled in the process and received favor. Esther won the prize gracefully.

Accept the next challenge. Faith allows us to be confident in knowing that He has orchestrated everything with our success in mind. We are often ripped away from what is comfortable during preparation, but it is necessary for our next level. When Esther was in the palace, she could only depend on God to prepare her for the position, which allowed her to be ready to fulfill her purpose. As a result, she prevented genocide of her day. God is preparing you for His own purposes and has you in a place where you can only rely on Him.

Esther's characteristics

Humility
Grace
Confidence
Determination
Focus
Beauty
Strength

Boldness

Obedience

Femininity

Kindness

Leadership

Reveal Your Inner Esther

There is an essence of Esther inside of each of us that makes us capable of similarly fulfilling our purpose. Esther sought God first because she recognized that the challenge that she faced was one of spiritual proportions. She recognized that her other gifts were ineffective, if not empowered by God's anointing. Similarly, our purpose is found at the intersection of our identity and our position. We find this place through self discovery and God's revelation. As God's children, we are called to go beyond the four walls of the church to impact society from a place of leadership. Is this a season of leadership development for you? Was this season in time uniquely penned for your existence? What is the time and season in your life? Focus outwardly with a critical eye in order to discover how your present relationships, finances, and status in your community are relevant to the world.

Esther did not use manipulation, but she used her own gifts, which she had prepared and sharpened, to increase the quality of life of other human beings. God is calling you to do the same—to reveal the Esther in you. You are so important that you can uniquely impact the world. Do you believe that you are ordained to change the course of human history? Will you step up to the challenge? You were created for such a time as this!

Affirmation: *"I am strong and beautiful, I am Esther!"*

Wisdom Challenge: Read the biblical book of Esther.

Reflection Questions:

What inspires you about Esther's story?

Which of Esther's qualities do you possess?

Which of Esther's qualities do you desire?

CHAPTER 2

PREGNANT WITH PURPOSE

"Before I formed you in the womb I knew you, before you were born I set you apart." Jeremiah 1:5 (NIV)

*P*rior to officially launching your personal Esther journey, it is important to realize your starting point—you are pregnant with purpose! God planted his purposes inside of you before he formed you in your mother's womb. You are not an accident and your life is not random. You were intentionally created as God's masterpiece. The same Great Designer of the Swiss Alps and the Grand Canyon designed you. Therefore, your life should be orchestrated by intentional steps daily to nurture the seeds of purpose within. Like an expectant mother, you are getting ready to give birth as you go through the gestation of your journey.

The foundational scripture for the Esther Project is found in Jeremiah 29:11, which you should commit to memory: "For I know the plans I have for you...plans to prosper you, give you a hope and a future." This scripture is particularly important because it proves a truth that is at your inner core—God has a plan for you. Similarly, Jeremiah 1:5 tells us, "Before I formed you in the womb I knew you, before you were born I set you apart." If He knew and formed us before we were in our mother's womb, then the essence of our life began before our human conception. The author of Psalm 139:13-16 stated, "You created my innermost being, you formed me in my mother's womb...your eyes saw my unformed body..." Similarly, the Apostle Paul remarked in his letter to the church in Rome that, "God knew his people in advance and chose them" (Romans 8:29). These scriptures confirm that His plan is to bring about his purposes that he planted inside of you before you were born.

Purpose is defined as an intended or desired result or the reason that something exists. We cannot escape our purpose because it is why we exist. We are also assured that God not only has a plan for us, but is giving us hope and a future. Hope is defined as the feeling that something desired will happen. We are intended to have hope. Therefore, we should not feel like things won't work out our way. In sum, God has impregnated us in the spirit with hope for a future, plans for good and prosperity, and he promises not to harm us.

So, what is the purpose of purpose? The seed of purpose is planted inside of each of us so that our divine destiny can be birthed. Purpose full blown becomes your destiny. The Esther Project is about that birthing process, with six phases that help us to move forward to our destiny. Before you endeavor to start the project, you must know WHO YOU ARE! Recognize that the Creator preexisted you, formed you, and knew you before you were in your mother's womb. He has a destiny and purpose for you that PRE-EXISTED YOU, which gives your life meaning that exceeds your natural desires to please only yourself. There is something in life to be experienced that goes beyond that which just brings pleasure to us. We must tap into what the will of God is for our lives. That is the essence of Jesus' prayer in the Garden of Gethsemane—"Not my will, but thy will be done" (Luke 22:42).

While you do not have to be a Christian to receive a benefit from this journey, its objectives will most optimally be fulfilled by your submission to the will of God in your life and a desire to have the Lord guide you towards his will. His will is that your purpose would come full grown to your destiny by taking steps to nurture that seed inside of us. This book will challenge you to give birth to your purpose through the following birthing phases:

1. Mastering the Fundamentals
2. Living on Purpose
3. Expanding Your Territory
4. Cocoon in the Wilderness
5. Breaking Forth
6. Taking Your Position

A Birthing Prerequisite: Say Good Night to Clutter!

The most important prerequisite to preparing for the birthing journey is to declutter, declutter, declutter! Removing clutter can entail physical items, relationships, thoughts, attitudes, and ideas. All should be fair game as you seek to fully prepare yourself for your purpose. I encourage you to organize your personal space, office, home, car, and closets by first removing items that are no longer useful or fitting for your "pregnancy." Clutter impacts your ability to function precisely and clearly. Your goal should be to create an environment that sets you up for success. What is your vision for how your home should be laid out, organized, maintained, or decorated? I doubt that you envision your dream home as having a messy garage, broken appliances, stained carpet, or books and mail scattered throughout your dining room table. Is it time to go through your closets and discard or donate items (only donate items in good condition) that are outdated, unflattering, damaged, and ill-fitting? How many coats, shoes, and accessories is it possible to use in one season? Consider sisters who are struggling to rebuild their lives who may be blessed by your donations.

As you begin your journey, removing clutter will ultimately help you focus on the task at hand without distraction. Esther was removed from her familiar environment to one that was free of distraction and filled with the necessities of her preparation process. Take the bold steps of transforming your personal space and relationships to allow the possibilities of your preparation to be endless!

Affirmation: *"I am pregnant with purpose—the salt of the earth and the light of the world. I will shine brightly every day."*

Wisdom Challenge: Read Jeremiah 1:5, 29:11 & "The Purpose Driven Life," by Rick Warren.

Reflection Questions:

Do you know why you are here? Does your daily routine reflect that you are operating in advancement of your purpose?

What are the areas of your life that are distracting you? Who are the people in your life that are distracting you?

What would you do differently if you allowed God to lead your daily decision-making?

CHAPTER 3

MASTERING THE FUNDAMENTALS

"Thank you for making me so wonderfully complex! Your workmanship is marvelous—how well I know it." Psalm 139:14 (NLT)

The first phase of the Esther Project focuses on grooming, pampering, personal presentation, and the art of self-care. Self-care is the hallmark of self-esteem, self-worth, and self-confidence. After all, when we look good, we feel good, and when we feel good, we are good. Our outward appearance reflects the manifestation of how we feel about ourselves, how we relate to others, and how we believe that we relate to the world. For example, if we are good hearted people inside, but disheveled outside, it may reflect that we think that other people's happiness is more important than ours. It could also reflect that we put other's needs before ours in an unbalanced way. More often than not, it reflects that we do not embrace and understand our value and worth in the world— that we have a unique role, power, and energy to impact positive global change. If from birth it were instilled that we were royalty, with a unique mission and purpose that only we could fulfill, our outward appearance and self-care would reflect our truth. We would not allow our exterior or interior to deteriorate or remain in a state of disrepair.

Ultimately, our view of ourselves, as reflected by how we care for ourselves, reflects our relationship with God. When we believe that we are fearfully and wonderfully made in God's image—so valuable that we were purchased with the ultimate price of Christ's death on the cross— our expression of that truth is reflected in the essence of how we present ourselves and care for ourselves. In life, we teach others how to treat us by how we present ourselves and conduct ourselves. When we encounter those with the highest regard for etiquette and protocol, we approach them gingerly, with grace and dignity, lest we should tarnish the standard that they have carefully laid out for themselves.

Many of you who are reading this are probably thinking, "Well, I know some pretty gorgeous atheists and some disappointingly slothful Christians!" To be clear, whether the outward shell is polished and manicured or not does not reflect whether someone has a relationship with Christ or whether they are going to heaven. Rather, the outward appearance can reflect our adherence to the truth of who God created us to be. After all, we are what He sees! It is my desire that through an increased and detailed routine of self-care, women would become closer to God by tapping into what they believe about who they are, embracing the truth of who they are, and reflecting that truth with confidence and assurance even by faith until it gets down in their heart and spirit.

During Esther's journey, she transformed her self-care routine. She was given specialized beauty treatments over the course of a year, to make her suitable for her role. Her treatments included elaborate baths in oil of myrrh for six months followed by another six month regiment of baths with perfumes and cosmetics. Esther also had a particularized diet plan along with proper rest and relaxation. I am confident that Esther was also physically examined to determine whether any physical imperfections needed to be corrected—including her face, teeth, hair, and frame. One fact that remained clear throughout Esther's journey was that her appearance and demeanor were pleasing to all those who laid eyes on her, which also caused her to have favor in their sight. We know that Esther outwardly exhibited her stunning inner beauty. Therefore, we do not exalt outer beauty over inner beauty, but we recognize that true beauty is the authentic beauty of boldly shining from within.

While you may not choose to pamper yourself in elaborate baths for 12 months (don't knock it till you've tried it!), consider the adjustments in your self-care routine that will ensure that you are suitably prepared for your future.

My Self-Care Journey

During my journey, I had to do the tough introspective once-over and assess my current self-care level. My findings were disturbing. I realized that I slept minimally, rarely ate throughout the day and as a result, ate junk food late at night. I rarely cooked or went grocery shopping, and my exercise routine was inconsistent. I often ignored doctor's appointments and physical ailments. My own meticulous grooming was often ignored because I was rushing to meet someone else's needs. The most revealing discovery was that I did not own a mirror in my home other than the bathroom mirror fixed to the wall. I realized that I had not purchased a mirror in over 10 years! I had often evaded looking at myself in the mirror and was not interested in assessing my appearance daily because I had been struggling with my body image, having never shed the extra 15+ pounds that I had gained since graduating law school and starting my professional career. No matter what the reflection in the mirror revealed, I always focused on my flaws and my perceived inability to control changing my reality. Feeling powerless to change, I resigned myself to a pattern of self-care that was self-defeating and sub-par.

The closer I drew to God through my Esther Project journey, the more I realized that my outward appearance and habits were a manifestation of an internal belief that I was not deserving of the truly fabulous and abundant life that God predestined me to live. As I began to awaken and look at myself, I decided to move forward and remember that I am important, too. I resolved that in my daily routine I would prioritize myself. So, as I am tempted to skip breakfast because I am running late for a Saturday morning commitment or grab my cosmetic bag to throw on my makeup later or try to skip a work out so I can get to work an hour early, I say out loud, "I am important, too."

The development of my daily routine and lifestyle of increased self-care remains challenging as I attempt to break habits developed through a flawed paradigm. Nonetheless, daily I resolve to value my life and the trust that I have been given. Secrets to my success thus far are attributable to generally living a more disciplined and scheduled life. I schedule everything from meals to flossing. I now take the time to spend more time with myself and learn myself. "Me time" is a non-negotiable, no matter who else in my life has to be disappointed that I am not dropping everything to support their needs. My journey to achieve the highest standard of self-care is continuous and perpetual.

I encourage you, Women of Esther, as you enter your journey to master the fundamentals, remember that you are important, too.

Affirmation: *I am important. God is relying on me to be a good steward and fulfill my purpose."*

Wisdom Challenge: Read a chapter of the book of Proverbs daily (journal its life application points) & "Commander in Chic" by Mikki Taylor.

Reflection Questions:

Are you satisfied with how you look and care for yourself? Why or why not?

Do you consider yourself an attractive person? Why or why not?

What does your appearance and grooming say to God and others?

CHAPTER 4

LIVING ON PURPOSE

"My purpose is to give them a rich and satisfying life." John 10:10 (NLT)

Living on purpose matters to God. An empty life is one in which every day is routine and without a sense of purpose, direction, and accountability. God wants us to live an abundant life. He created us to be fulfilled. We possess His essence—His Holy Spirit—which leads us to the truth of who we are and what we were created to accomplish. He has a plan and a predestined purpose for us. God sent his son Jesus to die for our sins so that we could live in eternity with Him. In the interim, He is preparing us for eternity and intends that we have an abundant life while we are living here on earth.

A life of purpose begins by knowing who you are and what God wants you to accomplish during your life. We have God-given signals of our purpose through our natural gifts, talents, and abilities. As we cultivate our natural gifts and offer them back to God, we will find fulfillment, direction, and belonging. By incorporating fun, enjoyment, and excitement into our lives, we become more interesting people that others will want to be around. As a result, our attitude and relationships will drastically improve. Art inspires beauty and expression. Exposure to different cultural stimuli leads us to a different understanding of ourselves and the world. It awakens our creativity, compelling us to interact with nature and express ourselves with unique abandon. We stop living in the "matrix" and free ourselves to be set apart as a unique individual, existing in the world but not a part of its paradigm.

However, enjoying life and developing passion can be challenging when you feel stagnant or stuck. We have to overcome what my father calls "lameness, sameness, and tameness" in our lives. These are the triplets of fear that represent complacency, laziness, and lack of motivation. These barriers will hold you back from living a fulfilled life unless you actively eradicate them from your daily lifestyle.

Esther Lived on Purpose

Esther lived on purpose through nurturing her natural gifting—her servant's heart, intelligence, charm, beauty, and grace—and moving out of her comfort zone by putting herself into consideration as a future queen. Esther fully embraced the preparation process and believed that she had the ability to surrender her life to the role of queen. She physically moved out of her comfort zone to an unfamiliar place and culture. Upon selection, Esther found peace and purpose in living her life as a queen and discovered a passion for justice. As queen, her passion propelled her to defy protocol and influence the king in reconsidering his edict to allow the destruction of the Jewish inhabitants.

Despite limited interaction with the king, Esther did not show signs of resentment, bitterness, or restlessness—nor did she complain about her role. In accepting her challenge, she prevented a racial genocide, preserved her own life, and discovered her purpose through the exhibition of her passion. As a result, we have her example to inspire us to discover our passion and nurture our natural gifts. Esther's story reminds us that we never know how God will use us to change the course of history just by using our passion.

My Journey to Live on Purpose

My story of living on purpose was that I realized that I had what I playfully call "no life." My life consisted of days packed with helping other people fulfill their dreams and nurturing their passions, but absolutely no attention to my own dreams and passions. I rarely went out socially unless it was a professional, sorority, or church related event. I failed to take time out to do activities that I enjoyed like dance, tennis, and cheering on my favorite football team, the New York Giants. I was rarely invited out because everyone perceived that I was busy and unavailable. Sadly, I realized that my circle of relationships had begun to consist solely of people who called on me primarily when they needed assistance. Although I was once a social butterfly, frequently hosting parties with lively games of Taboo and taking weekend jaunts to Newport, RI or Martha's Vineyard, those parties had ceased, those connections had waned, and the excursions were few and far between. As my personal frustration began to grow, it reached a climax when I realized that I was starting to resent the success of those who I had contributed to assisting. Rather than being proud and excited that they had achieved a goal to which I had contributed, I questioned God about why everyone else around me appeared to achieve their dreams to my exclusion.

Through my journey to live on purpose, I had to confront the truth of my feelings while accepting that their basic premise was based on an untruth. The truth was that I had not done so badly for myself either. In fact, I had been blessed with a series of professional accomplishments to rival someone twice my years of experience and had even achieved my childhood dream of becoming a judge, all by the age of 36. But I still had to confront the feeling that everyone was getting ahead except me. There was still an emptiness that would not go away despite my professional accomplishments. On a personal level, I still lacked the personal balance and relationships that sustained a fulfilled and enjoyable life. In my quest to be selfless, I realized that I had lost myself. I had reverted to a routine of being everyone's friend and had failed to demand friendship for myself. As my awareness changed, so did my social circle and the way in which I spent my time. New friends emerged and old relationships were redefined. Commitments to persons other than me reduced and took their proper order of priority—behind my own important priorities. I grappled with not becoming selfish but quickly realized that I had to rebalance and refill so that I could be effectively used to help others. My gratitude increased and my life contentment soared.

My deepest revelation was that my life was becoming full because God was changing me. He was grooming me to a place of leadership in ministry, which required meeting the needs of people in a different way than I had currently been functioning. While I had been actively working my ministry, He was starting something fresh. He was enabling me to minister to those around me. As He continued to mold and shape me, I learned that in order to meet the needs of others, I had to lead a life of purpose by example. My journey of discovering and remembering myself—through dreaming, getting out of my comfort zone, and traveling to different places—raised my awareness of the opportunity that was before me—to serve an incredible God. My dream is to bring the message of God's great love for humanity to the entire world through every communication means available. I will achieve this through continuing to incorporate fun, excitement, hobbies, good friends, and travel into my life. And yes, I believe I will resume those lively games of Taboo!

As you continue your journey, take inventory of your dreams and fuel your passions with exposure to new adventures. My quest to live on purpose has taken me to Paris, Rome, Greece, Belize, Mexico, St. Lucia, Bermuda, the Bahamas, Puerto Rico, Canada and coast to coast throughout the United States. I have many miles to go but I can truly say, I am living on purpose!

Affirmation: *"I enjoy life and have a passion to achieve the purpose that God planted inside of me."*

Wisdom Challenge: Read the books of James, Philippians & "Expect to Win" by Carla Harris.

Reflection Questions:

What is your dream job and what will it require to achieve it?

What are the areas in which you feel most successful and confident?

What are the qualities and attributes that you demonstrate in these areas that you can translate to areas where you feel least successful?

CHAPTER 5

EXPANDING YOUR TERRITORY

"Oh, that you would bless me and expand my territory! Please be with me
in all that I do, and keep me from all trouble and pain!"
I Chronicles 4:10 (NLT)

Stagnancy, complacency, and laziness—also known as lameness, sameness, and tameness— must be defeated in order to move forward toward God's purpose for your life. In sending his Son to die for humanity's sins, God intended that we would live an abundant life—a life of purpose. Our lives should be fun, exciting, and full of dreams of tomorrow while experiencing contentment of living in the moment. From the moment that we open our eyes upon waking and realize that we are still breathing, an awakening of hope and anticipation of what the day could bring should overpower us. Not only should our lives reflect thanksgiving for the activity of our limbs and neural power, we should endeavor to live as if we do not know if tomorrow will ever come. In truth, tomorrow is not promised and no man knows the day or the hour that the Lord is coming back to the earth for his church, ending life as we currently experience it. After having read the book of Revelation several times, I have a new appreciation for what life will be like here on earth for the unsaved during the Tribulation. Although I believe that I will be in heaven during this time, reading about the conditions of the earth post-Rapture gave me an enhanced urgency to spread the gospel to the entire world. My renewed desire to allow God to use me fully to fulfill his purposes has changed the paradigm of my life's vision.

God wants to use you fully to complete his purposes in you! He wants to start by moving you out of your comfort zone and to the next level. He is preparing you for future tasks and assignments that will bring you peace and fulfillment. He does not enjoy watching you live below your inheritance. Your destiny depends on your ability to live in your abundance. Abundance is not limited to personal financial wealth, but it also includes your inner peace, the quality of your relationships, your ability to use your resources, and your network of people. Who is in your network? What constitutes the territory of your current life? What will it take for you to expand your territory? Are you willing to follow God's leading?

First, expanding your territory requires feeling confident about yourself, knowing that you can go to the next level and succeed there. After having mastered the fundamentals, a better and more confident "you" results that others will be attracted to for any purpose that God sets forth. With greater confidence, you can master the task of obtaining divine connections through networking. Networking can seem intimidating as visions of extraverted and over-caffeinated overachievers may dance in your mind. However, consider how networking provides a challenge for you to discover who in the room possesses the resource to meet your need, and vice versa. Whose resource or answer are you holding?

Next, you have to simply take a step out of your comfort zone. There is far more reward than risk in taking the leap. Developing strong communication skills and mastering the art of conversation are vital tools to assist you in living a passionate and purposeful life. Marriages and relationships break down at alarming rates because of a lack of communication. Body language and subtle cues often speak louder than we intend if we are not controlled and deliberate in our communication. Emails, texts, and social media messages have replaced the beauty of face-to face dialogue and handwritten personal expressions. However, mastering the skill of effective communication will equip you with the tools to take the leap out of your comfort zone. Be assured that you will not fall flat on your face. As Dr. Martin Luther King Jr. eloquently stated, "faith is taking the first step even when you don't see the whole staircase."

My personal mountaintop experience

During my first visit to Vail, Colorado, I had what I call my personal mountaintop experience, which helped me to take the leap out of my comfort zone. I had an irrational fear of heights that I was determined to master. Vail reminded me of the stark natural beauty which inspired me to a greater revelation of who God is—regal, majestic, unmovable, distinct, exposed, accessible, life sustaining, life generating, revealed, captivating, inspiring, awesome, magnificent, and powerful. Hence I was reminded of my own identity, as I am a reflection of Him. I struggled with my fear of heights as I ascended to the mountaintop at 11,000 feet and embarked upon a snow shoeing hike. Being so close to the edge of the mountain on a narrow trail completely freaked me out! I kept having thoughts of falling off the side of the mountain and plunging to my death.

Through my gripping fear, I finally let go and asked God to just take my life in the palm of His capable hands and refocus my mind on the reality of my circumstances.

I realized in that moment that I released more than just my fear of heights, but something deeper had happened. Life looked different as I relaxed and took in the beauty around me. I began to cry as I felt the intimacy of the beauty of being so close to God. I realized that life was so much bigger than I had perceived and it was all in God's hands. I knew that I still needed to let go of my will and let God lead me. He is in control, and I have access to everything I need through Him. My mountaintop experience changed my life's perspective and identity. I realized who I was—the daughter of the King who created this universe.

Affirmation: *"I am God's ambassador, willing to go wherever He sends me to represent Him."*

Wisdom Challenge: Read the books of Ecclesiastes, Ephesians & "The Prayer of Jabez" by Bruce Wilkinson.

Reflection Questions:

In which areas of your life are you still in a comfort zone?

Which steps do you need to take that will represent a leap of faith towards the life you have dreamed?

When was the last time that you spent time with a group of people that you did not know well, doing something that you had never tried before?

When did you last take a walk or excursion to spend time with yourself and nature?

CHAPTER 6

COCOON IN THE WILDERNESS

"Now all glory to God, who is able, through his mighty power at work within us, to accomplish infinitely more than we might ask or think."
Ephesians 3:20 (NLT)

*J*ust like the children of Israel had their wilderness experience before entering the Promised Land, so must you! Esther encountered her wilderness experience as queen when she was challenged with having to request an audience with the king and plead for the lives of her people. Esther's response transformed her from a queen to a historic figure whose selfless act saved many lives. She found the promised land of her destiny through her metamorphosis. Your promised land and destiny awaits

A cocoon provides the safe encasing for the transformative process of a caterpillar to a butterfly. The cocoon can be susceptible to predators but is typically located in a remote and safe place—but not completely insulated from potential harm. In the cocoon, the caterpillar's juvenile systems are converted to adolescent systems. Wings are formed and a reproductive system develops. Similarly, in your cocoon, you will emerge with the ability to fly and reproduce yourself through a legacy of leadership. While your transformation may be shielded from public view, your cocoon could potentially be compromised prior to your total transformation. Becoming a cocoon in the wilderness requires faith that God will protect your cocoon and enable the maturation process to fully develop to completion. Only God, our creator, knows how to mature us precisely in the cocoon. His metamorphosis allows us to say "good night" to past hurts, pain, regret, and broken dreams. We cannot take this baggage with us once we emerge from the cocoon. Typically, a butterfly emerges from the cocoon in the morning. Esther, morning is coming! Allow God's healing balm to satiate the depths of your heart and allow him to remove the immature attitudes and develop the adult systems within you spiritually.

My cocoon in the wilderness phase came at a point in my career when I was unemployed after having resigned from a position. I was 30 years old, had recently purchased a home, and found myself in financial stress. After having initially envisioned a linear and accomplished career in the law, culminating in a judgeship, I now had to confront a bump in the road that propelled me off the track. The formulation of my cocoon's encasing began as my hope of a bright future in the legal profession had darkened and I was deeply depressed—crying regularly. I felt isolated and alone—like no one quite understood the depths of my pain and professional embarrassment at feeling like I had failed at my last position. I talked to very few people during this period of time with the exception of my immediate family, select church members, and few friends who reached out to support me.

As the cocoon had fully enveloped me, I began to feel the transformation. I could no longer rely on the faith and blessings of my parents' relationship with God. As the daughter of two pastors, I had long been the beneficiary of a legacy of comfort, love, and stability. I served God because I loved him, but also because it was what I grew up doing. I saw how God blessed my family and honored my parents' commitment to ministry. I considered myself a beneficiary of their relationship with Christ and His overflow of blessings to them. But I had not quite discovered God for myself. In my cocoon in the wilderness, I discovered that God was a provider because though I was in financial stress, I lacked nothing that I truly needed. I discovered that God was a comforter, because after I cried on the couch for two weeks, I suddenly felt a peace that surpassed my human understanding. I discovered that God was my best friend because He listened to me as I poured out my heart and He began to talk back—words of comfort and understanding, just like a best friend.

My greatest revelation was that God was calling me to serve Him. He gave me visions of speaking on His behalf, as His ambassador, meeting the needs of His people. He showed me who He had created me to be. I realized that I had limited my self-image to my past mistakes and sins—regretful decisions that were so heavy on my heart for which I thought God could never forgive, which I thought disqualified me to serve him. As I transformed in my cocoon, I surrendered to the metamorphosis process and let go of my past and trusted that God was preparing me for my future. So I accepted his calling and entered the ministry of Jesus Christ and preached my initial sermon one year after my cocoon in the wilderness process began.

God revealed himself as a restorer because within a few months of preaching my initial sermon, I accepted an offer to work at one of the largest and most prestigious law firms in my state. Within a year of starting, God blessed me with receiving four outstanding professional achievement awards in the two years that I was associated with the firm. I was eventually courted to serve as the Chief Counsel to the speaker of my state's legislature and later served as the Deputy Chief Counsel to the governor. Six years after my cocoon in the wilderness experience began with tears and sorrow, I had achieved my career goal of being appointed as a judge.

I credit my professional success to the glory of God being revealed in my life as I dedicated my life to His service. Before my cocoon in the wilderness experience, my ambition was to amass financial wealth and achieve professional success. As a result of my metamorphosis, I emerged with a passion to meet the needs of people through encouraging and inspiring them to live on purpose. In inspiring others to achieve their purpose, I achieve mine. My experience compelled me to conclude that we are interconnected in a chain of empowerment, sharing in one another's burdens and triumphs. My zeal and passion to fly to higher heights and duplicate my passion for service inspires me daily to strive for excellence. My cocoon was dark and lonely, but the transformation revealed the Esther inside of me. I was purposed to break forth through the cocoon and take my position. I discovered that I am strong and beautiful, and I am Esther!

As you focus on character development, transformation and faith walking, continue to be self-reflective, journal, and consider praying with an accountability partner. If you do not have a partner, consider selecting one immediately. Through this partnership, your barriers to listening and following God will be exposed, and as a result, these barriers will not continue to hold you back. I encourage you to be disciplined and dedicated so that you may be discipled by Christ.

Affirmation: *"I have God's favor and I expect that He will do exceedingly, abundantly more than I can ever think or ask."*

Wisdom Challenge: Read the books of Galatians, Romans, "The Battlefield of the Mind" by Joyce Meyer & "What's Really Holding You Back?" by Valorie Burton.

Reflection questions:

What is your greatest regret in life? Have you forgiven yourself?

Who do you need to forgive and from whom do you need to seek forgiveness? Consider taking the next step to draft an apology letter and send it.

What are your greatest strengths and areas of development? Consider selecting a theme scripture for your life.

What are your top 3 frustrations and top 3 goals for the next 3 months?

CHAPTER 7

BREAKING FORTH

"So I run with purpose in every step. I am not just shadowboxing. I discipline my body like an athlete, training it to do what it should. Otherwise, I fear that after preaching to others I myself might be disqualified."
I Corinthians 9:26-27 (NLT)

My personal challenge to break forth was rooted in battles with low self-esteem and poor body image. The symptoms of this problem manifested in several destructive habits in my life which I struggled to overcome including: emotional eating, lack of exercise, lack of financial fortitude, mindless TV watching, and not having enough fun. These symptoms were manifestations of a stronghold in my life which affected both my emotional and mental psyche, but I discovered that I could overcome through increased bible study, meditation, and yielding to the internal character work of the Holy Spirit. As a result, I began to incorporate the spiritual discipline of fasting, and I increased my prayer life. My breaking forth happened in the spirit, but I saw evidence in the natural.

More importantly, I knew that God had chosen me for a unique and powerful work here on earth—to encourage and inspire people to be all that He intended them to be. My purpose was to speak life into dead situations and to stir up complacency and lethargy—to energize stale environments and shatter the silence of the status quo with a piercing rally cry toward forward progress.

Breaking forth encouraged me to realize that the stronghold was only in my mind. It did not truly have the ability to limit me. It was a deceptive illusion of despair, poverty, and low self-esteem. Now, I have a vision from God of being a woman to whom people listen for advice and encouragement because my wise counsel is inspired by God's love for humanity. I see a woman of wisdom and an entrepreneur who knows how to "mind her business."

The Conversation in the Cave

In an effort to break forth, I decided to go on an adventure tour while visiting Belize, Central America, compliments of my best friend, Towanda Thorne, who was working as a diplomat in the country. I was told that the itinerary was cave tubing, hiking, and swimming at a natural bathing hole. Anyone who knows me can assure you that I normally would not choose to do any of these things unless it involved getting a spa treatment or shopping. However, my theme was getting out of my comfort zone. Not to mention that I have always had an apprehension of the dark. Yes, nightlights and lighted plug-ins have been staple items in my home. But I decided that one way that I would overcome this mental challenge was to embark upon cave tubing, which I understood to involve touring a dark cave on an inner tube.

The reality of the excursion still had not hit me as I prepared to get dressed that morning because Towanda and I argued over my attire. I put on my one-piece bathing suit, a sundress, and sandals which I thought was a compromise over the two-piece bathing suit, sarong, and the 3 1/2 inch open-toe python mules that I was originally going to wear. Towanda cautioned me that she thought that pants, sneakers, and something to cover my arms was more appropriate, along with plenty of insect repellent, given the elements in the cave. In my classic argumentative style, I dug in my heels, literally and figuratively. I don't own casual pants and only have one pair of jeans. Typically, I would never be seen with sneakers on as part of an outfit, and all of my other shoes are stilettos or boots. Finally, I emerged wearing a pair of cargo capris, a sleeveless ruffled python printed shirt, and sneakers. I opted to put the insect repellant, flip flops, towel, and a change of clothes in the large brown Coach bag that was doubling as my knapsack for the day.

Off I went to meet my personal tour guide, Marcos. After some confusion about which side of the bus depot parking lot that he was parked in, Marcos emerged from a lime green pick-up truck ready to escort me to my break through. I sized up Marcos and the condition of the truck in approximately 30 seconds and decided it was a go. After all, I am a single woman in a strange land going to tour a dark, remote cave with a strange man who I had never met before. I had doubts about whether this was a smart idea, but I pressed on anyway. I figured it would be a great story for my Lifetime biography if things didn't work out (morbid, I know.) As we rode down Hummingbird Highway and Marcos gave me the history of the area's devastation during the last hurricane, I begin to feel at ease.

After about 20 minutes, we arrived at the area where we were starting the hike to the cave. There was a narrow path through thick brush which I realized was really the jungle. Marcos stops at a paw print and notes that a "cat" must be in the area but that I should not worry because, based on the size of the paw print, it was only 35-50 lbs, which was of no concern because it was smaller than a jaguar. Great, I really feel at ease now, Marcos. Really assured that this was probably the best decision I have ever made. The dense trees are magnificent and regal, but I still can't quite stop thinking about the fact that I have no idea what is in them, watching me. So this relaxing hike is elevating my heart rate, and I am really out of my comfort zone.

We arrive at the cave, and I knew that there was no turning back at this point. So I sucked it up and start descending the steps to the cave as Marcos shared that he was of Mayan ancestry and that the caves were sacred to Mayan culture. The caves represented the 9 levels of the underworld which Mayans believed that they had to go through and conqueror. The caves were used for ceremonies, and I was aware that this included human sacrifice—only adding to the "ambience" of the pitch black cave. Marcos gave me the warning that there were bats in the cave as well but that they wouldn't bother us. Uhmm-hmm. Keep talking Marcos. I will be running from here in my sneakers in about 60 seconds flat the moment a bat shows up.

The cave was darker than I suspected, and I guess I didn't realize that literally there was no electricity in there! Marcos gave me a hard hat with a light attached to it. Again, I'm really suffering here because the only thing I hate more than sneakers is a hat. But I digress. I don my hardhat with the light, and we are off, down the steps into the cave. As I reached the bottom of the steps, I noticed that a beautiful river ran through it. I turned around and looked at the entrance to the cave and observed the most beautiful sight. The greenery mixed with the rocks, cascading down to the river with the sunlight glistening, looked absolutely breathtaking. I felt like I was on the set of a movie. I was inspired to continue on and discover more of nature's offerings.

I decided that my strategy would be "less is more." The less I actually saw in the cave, the more likely I would be not to pass out. Quickly, I realized that I would not just be walking in the cave or tubing effortlessly down the river. Navigating the cave required climbing, hoisting, jumping, stretching, and full muscular engagement. At the point that I found myself on my belly sliding under a narrow area of rock and then flipping over to slide on my back in order to reach the next foothold, I became acutely aware of why wearing a dress and mules would not have been a wise choice. At some point, something within me kicked in and said, "This is actually fun, an adventure, and great exercise." Marcos and I began to talk about our lives, and he shared that he struggled with maintaining his cultural identity yet serving God. His strong Christian parents rejected Mayan culture as contrary to God's dictates, but he struggled with a sense of lost identity that he wanted to share with his children and embrace for himself. While he did not agree with all of Mayan spiritual beliefs, he believed that history was important to preserve in his family. I pondered his words, his sincerity, and his passion and thought about the similar quandary that I find myself in when I reflect on many pagan cultural traditions of African ancestors that I do not embrace spiritually. Yet I feel an obligation to know and understand my identity and where I come from culturally. I assured Marcos that in order to raise empowered children who knew how to make good choices, they had to know their history and identity. We both agreed that knowledge of history was the key to avoiding the mistakes of the past.

As we ventured on through the cave, which got narrower and darker with each step, our conversation got deeper and more reflective. I told Marcos about my Esther Project and the journey that I was on personally. I shared that this excursion was a part of my journey to step outside of my comfort zone and gain mental strength and courage that I knew existed but that I did not exercise or embrace. I followed his footsteps through every hill and valley and was reminded that this is how I have to follow Christ. It may be unfamiliar, daunting, and even dark, but the Holy Spirit serves as a light, a familiar guide, and a companion. My "aha" moment, Oprah.

Excitement began to build and my pace began to quicken as I leaped and climbed and jumped and crawled, maneuvering passageways that looked impassable by human foot. I realized that so goes the journey of my destiny. We finally arrived at the furthest point in the cave that was passable—the upper chamber where sacred Mayan ceremonies were performed. The natural rock formation hanging from the ceiling was majestic and magnificent, particularly as the limestone's glints of gold and silver glitter glistened brightly with each ray of light from our head lamps. It was breathtaking and reiterated the majesty of the Divine Creator and Great Designer. As Marcos and I took in the beauty, we continued our conversation about life. I shared my vision of traveling the world, sharing about the Lord, and empowering women through my Esther Project. I told him that I also aspired to take on the world's stage through expressing my message on television. As I spoke, I noticed that my passion caused my cadence to increase and the energy in my body to exude until the hairs on my neck were standing straight up. Even though we were in a cave, there was a fresh wind. When I stopped speaking, I literally looked at myself and said, "Who is this woman?" I never knew her. Well, I used to know her, and I am glad that she is back.

Marcos shared about his deep devotion to his children, yet his frustration at being separated from his wife of 16 years. His hurt and pain echoed along the walls of the cavern as I witnessed a man who was at a crossroads, caught between responsibility and passion. He shared that his marriage broke up because his wife did not like his work as an expedition leader and guide. At first, I did not understand why she would be concerned, then I realized that yes, it must take an extraordinarily secure woman to trust her husband daily as he leads beautiful women into dark caves! I began to pray silently for Marcos as he poured out his heart. We talked about his relationship with his daughter which was growing strained due to the dynamics of the separation. I shared with him the model of mentoring from my girls' leadership academy, and I suggested that he find women in the community that could mentor his daughter in different areas of life. I encouraged him to take her to these women's jobs and let her see what they do and experience a day in their life.

We must have talked for at least 45 minutes. As Marcos pondered his next step for his family and as I pondered my dreams, we both silently recognized that through our conversation in the cave, we had crossed a mental divide that had been a Red Sea in our lives. We had walked over the sea on dry land and were on our journey to our promised land. We left the chamber and tubed back to the cave entrance with a new energy. I was relaxed and didn't even let the bats that flew overhead concern me. I was too preoccupied with what I would do once I left the cave. I knew that a new day had dawned and that God had an incredible work for me to do. I was convinced more than ever that I was walking in my destiny. God knew that I would need that conversation in the cave when he created me. He already foresaw that I would get to a point in my life's journey where I had lost myself and my true purpose. He knew that I would put on the weight of the world and cover myself with the protective barriers that life's circumstances drove me to secure. But when I emerged from the cave, I was a new woman. Invincible, unstoppable, and undeniable. I know my identity. I am strong and beautiful, I am Esther!

Affirmation: *"I can achieve all things through Christ and nothing is impossible to me."*

Wisdom Challenge: Read the books of I Corinthians, II Corinthians, "The Daniel Plan" by Rick Warren & "The 21 Day Financial Fast" by Michelle Singletary.

Reflection Questions:

In which areas of your life do you honestly need to break forth?

How would you rate your commitment to a healthy lifestyle on a scale of 1–10? How often do you engage in physical exercise?

Do you consider yourself disciplined in your spending and budgeting? Do you have a plan that is effectively propelling you towards your envisioned future financially?

CHAPTER 8

TAKING YOUR POSITION

"Therefore, go and make disciples of all the nations, baptizing them in the
name of the Father and the Son and the Holy Spirit. Teach these new
disciples to obey all the commands I have given you. And be sure of this:
I am with you always, even to the end of the age."
Matthew 28:19-20 (NLT)

Preparation meets opportunity at the intersection of your position. Positioning yourself is vital to fulfilling your purpose. Many people live a life that is continually preparing for what could be, but not actually positioning themselves for their potential to become a reality. A perpetual dream unfulfilled could be considered a hallucination or a fantasy after a while. God intended that our lives be purposeful and intentional. While we begin with a dream in our hearts and a vision in our minds, our prepatory steps lead us to the moment when we must jump off the cliff and take our position. The position of purpose does not have a linear roadmap or a well lit directional sign. Neither does it appear to be the glamorous life of the rich and famous. Being a leader does not entail a life of being served, but rather it requires the highest form of personal service and self-sacrifice.

Taking your position requires an evaluation of the reality of leadership. A leader must bring resources to problems. Therefore, a leader must be close to the real life experiences of people as well as accessible to elite circles of influence and wealth. Another stark reality is that leading can be lonely and isolating at times. Leaders are often misunderstood, scorned, mocked, and ridiculed. Consider Joseph who was mocked by his brothers and eventually sold by them into slavery because of their jealousy of his gift of leadership. King David was also ridiculed and belittled by his own brothers when he stepped onto the battlefield to declare that he would slay Goliath. Esther had to leave her entire social circle behind in order to take the position of queen. She no longer had the same confidantes and could no longer share the same conversation with her same friends. Jesus was mocked, scorned, and falsely accused in the exercise of his leadership authority. All of these leaders had strong faith in God who equipped them to deal with the interpersonal dynamics of leadership, which did not ultimately dissuade them from accomplishing their missions. Effective leadership is not contingent upon being well-liked or popular, but instead is premised upon strict obedience to completing the mission. Your faith and yielding to God's priorities for your life will allow you to be mission-minded and complete your God-inspired work.

I often reflect on the professional leadership building experiences that shaped my ability to lead other women into a realization of their God-given purpose. I gained the courage to take my position through the love and spiritual guidance of my parents, Bruce and Phyllis Williams, who are also my pastors. Their parenting style was one of structure, support, and an emphasis on achieving personal excellence. As pastors, they taught me to see people the way Christ sees them and to patiently make decisions that are inspired by God's calling on my life. The greatest leadership values that have been passed in legacy to me are service, compassion, integrity, courage, boldness, responsibility, and acceptance. As a result, my foundation was set without a flaw. Even as my youthful transgressions attempted to chip away at the integrity of the foundation, it did not give way because, as the old hymn by Edward Mote says, "my hope is built on nothing less than Jesus' blood and righteousness. I dare not trust the sweetest frame but wholly lean on Jesus' name. On Christ the solid rock I stand, all other ground is sinking sand."

At times in my journey, I could not understand why my perspective was so different from everyone else in my environment. I was often frustrated that they could not see the same vision that I saw. After many venting sessions and self-doubt as to whether I was cut out to lead, I discovered the peace of taking my position. I accepted that I was uniquely suited to solve the problems that arose in my environment. I tapped into my vast resource network to add value to others and make their tasks easier. I noticed that as my personal leadership touched others, my influence and authority grew. I began to own my leadership style and exhibit it with greater confidence. As a result, I was ready when the opportunity arose to dare to create my own platform from which to empower others. While new leadership challenges arise daily, I am equipped to look at my past successes and failures as a barometer that I am moving forward.

God is equipping you to take your position as a leader upon whom he can rely to bring resources to the world. He cares for the world and uses his people to meet the world's needs. In fulfilling our purpose and sharing the love of Christ, God gives us a model of how to develop disciples that will open themselves up to follow him. The circle of eternal love is linked through willing hands that can change the course of human history. We are links in the chain if we will dare to take our position. Are you up to the challenge?

Affirmation: *"I am a virtuous woman created to take my position of purpose and leave a legacy of hope for others. I will lift as I climb."*

Wisdom Challenge: Read Proverbs 31, Judges 4, "Successful Women Think Differently," by Valorie Burton & "Developing the Leader Within," by John Maxwell.

Reflection Questions:

Which leadership qualities do you most need to develop? What steps are you willing to take to sharpen your saw?

Who can you mentor, teach, and lift as you climb? When will you start?

Where are people in need of your gifts and talents? How can you reach them?

How can you build a platform from which you can share your gift of leadership? What resources are available to assist you with a first step?

EPILOGUE

THE GENESIS

"For I am about to do something new. See, I have already begun!
Do you not see it? I will make a pathway through the wilderness.
I will create rivers in the dry wasteland."
Isaiah 43:19 (NLT)

The journey towards living a life of passion and purpose is truly the beginning of a new life...a genesis. I encourage you to realize that living a life of epic proportions is merely a personal decision. The contours of your life up until this very moment are propelling you forward. Through your fears and vulnerabilities, you can apply the lessons and rise like the phoenix from the ashes. The genesis has begun, and it requires a new mindset, a new vision, and a new image. Are you destined to accomplish feats of historic proportions by living boldly and courageously? Value the journey of preparation which allows you to position yourself for your purpose.

Preparation...position...purpose. Identify and connect with Esthers in your own community and strive to become an Esther that can be a role model to a younger sister. Reveal your Esther and set the world ablaze! You are strong and beautiful...you are Esther!

"Our deepest fear is not that we are inadequate. Our deepest fear is that we are powerful beyond measure. It is our light, not our darkness that most frightens us. We ask ourselves, Who am I to be brilliant, gorgeous, talented, and fabulous? Actually, who are you not to be? You are a child of God. Your playing small does not serve the world. There is nothing enlightened about shrinking so that other people will not feel insecure around you. We are all meant to shine, as children do. We were born to make manifest the glory of God that is within us. It is not just in some of us; it is in everyone and as we let our own light shine, we unconsciously give others permission to do the same. As we are liberated from our own fear, our presence automatically liberates others."

Marianne Williamson, excerpted from Return to Love, HarperCollins, 1992.

If you are motivated to begin a journey of purpose and passion, I encourage you to turn the page and begin a dedicated six-month journey using the Esther Project Challenge materials found in the Appendix. I encourage you to take the journey with an accountability partner or initiate an entire empowerment circle of women to take the challenge together. Visit our website www.iamesther.org or contact us at info@iamesther.org to obtain a copy of our Esther Project Challenge Workbook, Facilitator's Guide or Esther Girls Challenge.

APPENDIX

THE ESTHER PROJECT CHALLENGE

Welcome to the Esther Project Challenge!

I believe that every woman is "pregnant with purpose," and this personal journey of empowerment will allow you to nourish your inner seeds of purpose. The project's inspiration, Esther, was a young queen who prepared herself for her role and encountered a deeper purpose once she arrived in her position. As queen, she used her influence to save an entire race from genocide.

Esther reminds and inspires women to prepare themselves, get in position and uncover their purpose. The challenges are included in these materials, along with a companion reading plan, journal questions and affirmations for each project phase. I encourage you to connect with an accountability partner and consider forming an Esther Empowerment Circle. I invite you to embark upon your personal journey of self-empowerment, self-discovery and spiritual advancement towards your purpose.

Project Phase	Project Focus	Project Challenges
Phase 1 Mastering the Fundamentals	Grooming, presentation, self-care	**Week 1—Pamper your sleep** Commit to 7-8 hours of sleep nightly. Obtain quality, high thread count sheets, and feminine pajamas. Create a queen's throne bed. **Week 2—Pamper your teeth** Schedule a 6-month check up with dentist. Change toothbrush, floss 3x's daily, mouthwash, mints, whitening agent. Schedule an appointment to resolve any issues that detract from your smile! **Week 3—Pamper your skin** Enjoy a luxurious bath 2-3x's with bath salts, body scrubs, bath oil, bath pillow. Replace worn towels with high quality, fluffy, absorbent, bath sized. Obtain skin care essentials Schedule a facial this month. Schedule a dermatologist appointment. **Week 4—Back to the basics** Develop a morning and night pampering routine. Develop a weekly/monthly schedule for grooming appointments—hair styling, hair removal, manicures, pedicures, massage.
Phase 2 Living on Purpose	Passion, dreaming, life enjoyment	**Week 1**—Plan a cultural, arts or sports event outing to attend this month. Invite a young woman that you would like to mentor. **Week 2**—Plan a day trip to take next month. **Week 3**—Plan a vacation for next year. **Week 4**—Create a vision board with images of who you want to become, what you want to have, where you want to live, or where you want to vacation.
Phase 3 Expanding Your Territory	Networking, mmunications, relationship-building	**Week 1**—Meet 3 new people this week and exchange contact information. **Week 2**—Attend an event or outing that is out of your comfort zone and meet at least one new person. **Week 3**—Initiate a group outing or activity with at least 3 others (movie outing, skating, bowling, dinner). **Week 4**—Host a small gathering with at least 4 participants & share the Project. Share your journey & invite them to take the challenge.

Phase 4 Cocoon in the Wilderness	Character development, faith-walking, transformation	Journal responses to the following questions and select a prayer partner that will be committed to pray with you weekly about the revelations from your journaling **Week 1**—What are your greatest strengths & greatest areas of development? Select a theme scripture for your life. **Week 2**—What is your biggest regret in life? What is a step that you are willing to take to turn this regret into a victory or teachable movement? **Week 3**—Who are people in your life that you need to forgive or whose forgiveness are you seeking? Consider letting go of those who deeply hurt you by making an oral declaration to your prayer partner. **Week 4**—What are 5 small goals that you will achieve in the next 3 months?
Phase 5 Breaking Forth	Developing emotional, mental and physical strength	**10 days of reflection** — Establish 30 minutes of quiet time daily to reflect on your greatest personal/emotional needs. Listen to what God may be saying to you about this area of your life. **10 day of healthy choices** – Commit to consuming foods nourishing to your body. Where can you choose a healthier way of cooking. Get moving by walking or exercising at least 15 min every day. Add 15 min daily if you're already exercising. Journal your fitness goals; take a photo. **10 days of financial empowerment**—Consider turning a skill into a business opportunity or identify a new skill to develop. Develop or revise your monthly budget to reflect your financial priorities. Consider developing a spreadsheet to track your monthly spending and projections for the entire year. Establish at least 3 short term and 3 long term financial goals.
Phase 6 Taking Your Position	Leadership development, empowering others, legacy building	**Week 1**—Find a young girl to share advice and wisdom on becoming a woman. Spend at least 1-2 hours with her monthly. **Week 2-3**—Develop a life plan including your top 3 goals in the next year, 5yrs and 10 yrs, encompassing every area of your life (family, career, health, education, etc.). Your plan should include your ideal vision of the priority areas of your life, your current state of reality and an action plan of how to achieve your vision for each area. **Week 4**—Draft a 1 page testimonial about your Esther Project journey and email us at info@iamesther.org.

Project Wisdom Challenges

During the journey, biblical readings and journal questions are assigned in order to offer a biblical foundation for each phase. It is important not to ignore these wisdom challenges because they are crucial to your success in nurturing your seeds of purpose. I encourage you to journal the life application points inspired by the reading daily. Additionally, consider the journal questions below.

Reading Plan		Journal Questions
Pre-Challenge	Esther	What inspires you about Esther's story? Which of Esther's qualities do you possess or desire?
Phase 1	Proverbs Read a chapter daily	How wise do you consider yourself? Why? How can you increase your wisdom in daily decision making?
Phase 2	James (weeks 1-2) Philippians (weeks 3-4)	How can you reflect more joy in your life through your attitude and actions? What are you doing to draw closer to God?
Phase 3	Ecclesiastes (weeks 1-2) Ephesians (weeks 3-4)	How would you describe your present "time and season"? How does the armor of God help you in your daily journey?
Phase 4	Galatians (weeks 1-2) Romans (weeks 3-4)	How do you exhibit the fruit of the spirit in your life? How would you rate your level of faith? How do you walk by faith in your life?

Phase 5	I Corinthians (weeks 1-2)	What does a Godly lifestyle consist of?
	II Corinthians (weeks 3-4)	How does your life reflect God's standards? Are there any negative behaviors that you need to release?
Phase 6	Proverbs 31 (weeks 1-2)	How would you compare yourself to the virtuous woman? How would you describe yourself?
	Judges 4 (weeks 3-4)	What inspires you about Deborah's story?

Project Affirmations

Speaking the truth over your circumstances is transformational and visionary. It takes courage and faith to "act as if" your dream is already a reality. Esther spoke life and truth into her future and her circumstances began to reflect her confession. During the journey, I encourage you to speak forth the truth about yourself, your circumstances, and your future. Below, I have developed sample affirmations for each phase in order to keep you motivated and focused on uncovering your purpose.

Phase 1	"I am important. God is relying on me to be a good steward and fulfill my purpose."
Phase 2	"I enjoy life and have a passion to achieve the purpose that God planted inside of me."
Phase 3	"I am God's ambassador, willing to go wherever He sends me to represent Him."
Phase 4	"I have God's favor and I expect that He will do exceedingly abundantly more than I can ever think or ask."
Phase 5	"I am strong and beautiful. I can achieve all things through Christ and nothing is impossible to me."
Phase 6	"I am a virtuous woman created to take my position of purpose and leave a legacy of hope for others. I will lift as I climb."

Contact Us

We would love to connect you to the women of the Esther Project and invite you to consider joining our empowerment movement. Additionally, we can assist you in forming an empowerment circle of sisters in your area and keep you engaged and motivated in preparing for your purpose. For further information on our sisterhood and upcoming events, seminars, and conferences, or to request a presentation of the Esther Project to your group of women or girls, contact us at info@ iamesther.org. To download a pdf version of the Challenge for women or girls, visit our website at www.iamesther.org.